The Noble Wilds

The Supreme Master Ching Hai

Foreword

*I*n the animal kingdom, size doesn't matter and virtues count like everywhere else.

Thus, I have discovered for example that the tiny squirrels have individual names but the ducks don't.

That may be due to the fact that squirrels have higher NQ (Noble Quality) than the ducks.

I have also discovered that if a race of animal possesses an NQ of 9% or higher, it will be entitled by nature to have an individual name!
(The human is more privileged.)

Here are some for general reference:

Cows = 40%	Some birds = 30%
Elephants =30%	Coots = 10%
Pigs = 30%	Beavers = 10%
Deer = 20%	Swans = 20 %
Dogs = 30%	Geese = 20 %
Eagles = 3%	Orangutans = 20%
Squirrels = 10%	Tigers = 4%
Duck = 8%	Lions = 3%

Humans:
High = 90% (small number)
Low = 3% (lots)
Average = 10% (lots)

I've also learnt that animal parents don't give names to their offspring, but it will be transmitted to them in time by the council of their species. For example, swans will "pick up" their names before maturity, around two years of age; the same with geese, and in the case of beaver or squirrel, around one year.

Some animals of the same species have more NQ on average than others,
For example:

Pitu = 30%, Female Swan
Gina = 25%, Female Swan

Only among humans, the NQ varies greatly because we are more equipped to develop compassion; also we are more exposed to different situations, which require our love and help for other fellow humans and other beings.

Yes! I was also surprised by the finding! There are so many marvels even in this physical universe. One really must take time to discover.

And another thing: Female animals in general have 1 or 2% higher NQ than their male counterpart, and in the human world it's the same. I guess motherhood does help to develop more unconditional love, and the more one exercises "NQ," the more extra one will have.

It is a privilege for me to be revealed this information. I did not seek to know. It just came by itself as the bond of friendship deepened between the wilds and I. Once I knew some of them, other species' data became also available. Once we know even as little as what I know, we will never look at the animals the same way as we did before.

I am very happy to share a little knowledge about some of our co-inhabitants in this book. Some of those whom, as language barriers prevent us to understand each other, have been mistreated, misused or forgotten.

If I were to write much more of what has been transmitted from them, it will take many books; besides, it only concerns myself and others I need to be in contact with as part of my "job's" necessity. So I do not include herein.

Anyway, I was thrilled to know much about our animal friends; hope you too will be.

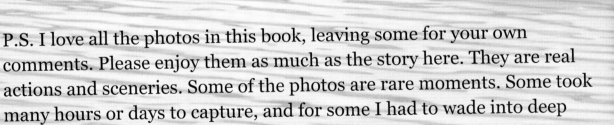

May all beings be loved and blessed - with Peace & Happiness.

P.S. I love all the photos in this book, leaving some for your own comments. Please enjoy them as much as the story here. They are real actions and sceneries. Some of the photos are rare moments. Some took many hours or days to capture, and for some I had to wade into deep water or thick forest to film... (Video & photos)

Appreciation

This book is about the wilds, but I also feel like a "wild" myself. Though is not about me, but you see my photo sometimes. I think you like it, no? Thanks to several assistants who caught my image for you:

Thomas Lerning   T. Hao
T. June   Steve Andreas
Jus-se   T. Khai

For the rest of the pictures and sceneries, you'll have to bear it without the old woman. But I am always there with you, behind the camera.

There are more residents and tourists who are not in the book: The big fishes, frogs, tortoises, rabbits, owls, pigeons, different birds, crickets, snails, deer, etc... But I thank them all for their love and support, so that this book can reach you.

I can take photos and write forever; maybe I will, because they all are fascinating. For example: As I camp near by, the frogs chorused all night, singing, responding back and forth till dawn, sometimes longer. It's like a perfectly orchestrated musical performance, free and nonstop; who gives them such magnificent voice and robust energy? And in such a size so tiny!

On the other hand, maybe I let you polish your imagination a little or go click the camera yourself.

I love writing this special book.

I love all beings in this book and all others.

I love all the sceneries that I photographed.

I love the feeling that you will read and enjoy.

Specially
Dedicated lovingly to :
Gina   Moruwey
Pitu   Sai Sai

And thank you for your love and help
Thank you for your permission to photograph and write this book about
you, even in your intimate residence.

> You have come from far away,
> To be my friends
> And my willing assistants!
> Your loving comfort,
> Your precious wisdom...
>
> I just wish the world can understand
> I just wish the world can feel the love that
>   radiates from your being
> I will always cherish
> The gift of your presence
> Whether you choose to leave
> Or (of course it is better) to stay.

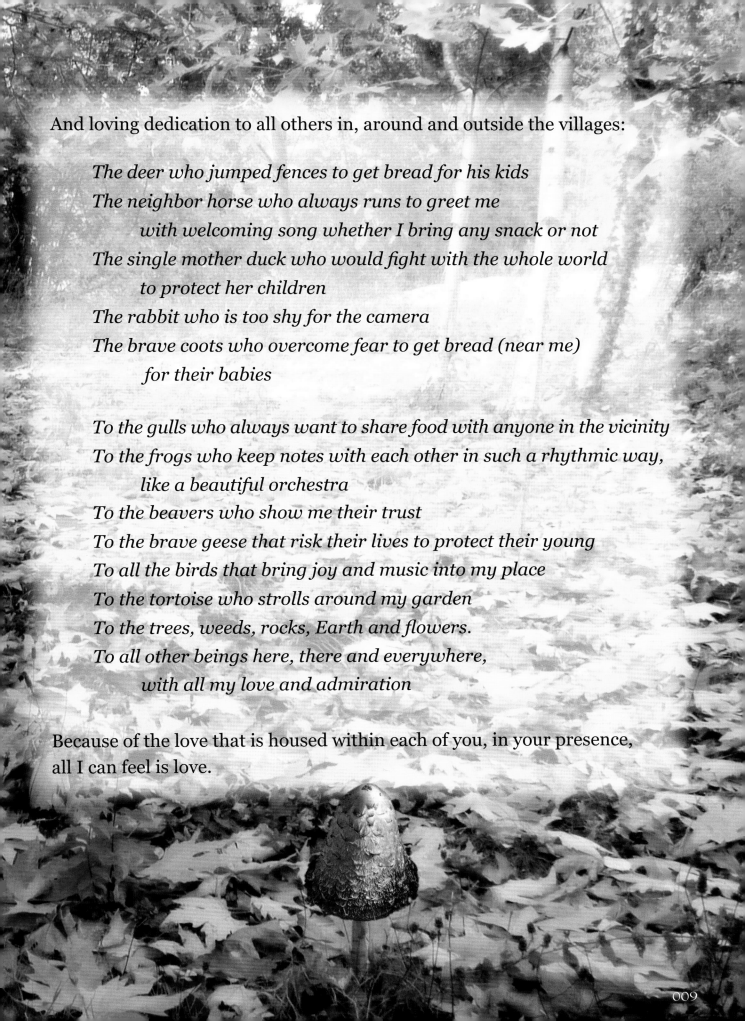

And loving dedication to all others in, around and outside the villages:

> The deer who jumped fences to get bread for his kids
> The neighbor horse who always runs to greet me
> > with welcoming song whether I bring any snack or not
> The single mother duck who would fight with the whole world
> > to protect her children
> The rabbit who is too shy for the camera
> The brave coots who overcome fear to get bread (near me)
> > for their babies

> To the gulls who always want to share food with anyone in the vicinity
> To the frogs who keep notes with each other in such a rhythmic way,
> > like a beautiful orchestra
> To the beavers who show me their trust
> To the brave geese that risk their lives to protect their young
> To all the birds that bring joy and music into my place
> To the tortoise who strolls around my garden
> To the trees, weeds, rocks, Earth and flowers.
> To all other beings here, there and everywhere,
> > with all my love and admiration

Because of the love that is housed within each of you, in your presence,
all I can feel is love.

And a final dedication to the little swan baby who left me while I was conducting a retreat overseas:

I would have loved to say "I missed you" when I came back. I would have loved to see you grow big like your brothers & sisters. I felt a frustrating sadness not having been there to protect you.

Though I know you are better in Heaven, still I can't say that I am so detached and cold.

This book is partly for you: the cute, lovely chick that was too fragile for the harsh wildness of this world.

> *I would have loved to feed you*
> > *till you are old enough to fly away free.*
> *I would have loved to hug you*
> *Though you know I would never do it.*
> *I would have loved to feel your silky feathers*
> *Though I know I would never try.*
> *'Cause I respect your free wild nature*
> *And the unconditional bond between you and I.*

I want to love you just as your parents love you:
Just take care of you, then let you go. But oh not so soon like that,
in your tender days of a baby. I do know Heaven has plans, and I do know
Heaven welcomed you as "The way it is." But I still miss you, as if my
child has been lost. You were so little, so helpless; you hadn't even got a
name...

Farewell baby, I love you dearly, and you know it from above. As I am
writing about you now, do you see my tears flow?

Maybe I will remember you as "Princess Love."
Because that's what you are.
Because that's what the rest of YOU animals are: Love.
And I love you all deeply.
How deep, only I alone know!

Supreme Master Ching Hai

With a rhythmic, meditative tone, the words of *The Noble Wilds* flow gracefully along the pages, complemented by the luminous photos of God's creations in nature. Turning the pages, one is transported to Amoura, the place where "the lady" lives and is visited by cherished beings of the wild.

The "lady" is none other than Supreme Master Ching Hai, and *The Noble Wilds* is yet another of Her simple but deeply touching gifts. Written, photographed and compiled personally by Master, this precious gem opens the door to a world of unique beauty. Here, the reader can witness first-hand the noble spirit and dedication of our co-inhabitants whose homes are under the open sky —the swan, the goose, the squirrel, the beaver and even a tiny garden snail. Although generally shy of humans, these animals allow themselves to be photographed, and indeed can even be seen eagerly approaching "the lady's" gentle offering of favorite foods. The love conveyed is unlike any other — full of dignity and grace, yet as deep and enduring as the eternal.

We wish that the treasured reader may become ever more absorbed in this enrapturing tale as it unfolds with each page of *The Noble Wilds*. And finally, our deepest appreciation to our beloved Master, for You have shown us how to appreciate the beauty of the natural world and the most treasured qualities of her inhabitants.

Compiled by Books Group

Master expresses Her sincere thanks to the following persons for their diligence and love throughout the making of this book:

Kim Joung Eun, Gary Lai, Annie Yu, Jackie, Cuties, Pearl Huang, Nadir Yen, Eve Lin (Designer and Layout)

Gary Lai, Kim Joung Eun, Wang Bor Tang, Yu Hui-Chun, Nadir Yen (Graphic Design)

Jane Chu, Lynn McGee, Grace Chen, Sun Wang (Copy Proofreading)

Biography of The Supreme Master Ching Hai

The Supreme Master Ching Hai was born in Central Au Lac (Vietnam). At the age of eighteen, Master Ching Hai moved to England to study, and then later to France and then Germany, where She worked for the Red Cross and married a German physician. After two years of happy marriage, with Her husband's blessings, She left Her marriage in pursuit of enlightenment, thus fulfilling an ideal that had been with Her since Her childhood. This began a time of arduous pilgrimages to many different countries that ended only when She met a perfect living Master in the Himalayas. Master Ching Hai received the divine transmission of the inner Light and Sound, which She later called the Quan Yin Method. After a period of diligent practice, She attained Perfect Enlightenment.

To satisfy the longing of sincere Truth seekers, the Supreme Master Ching Hai offers the Quan Yin Method of meditation to people of all nationalities, religions and cultural backgrounds. Her message of love and peace brings spiritual liberation and hope to people throughout the world, reminding all to uphold Truth, Virtue, and Beauty in life.

Contents

In speaking of God or the Supreme Spirit, Master instructs us to use original non-sexist terms to avoid the argument about whether God is a She or a He.
She + He = Hes (as in Bless)
Her + Him = Hirm (as in Firm)
Hers + His = Hiers (as in Dear)
Example: When God wishes, Hes makes things happen according to Hiers will to suit Hirmself.

As a creator of artistic designs as well as a spiritual teacher, Supreme Master Ching Hai loves all expressions of inner beauty. It is for this reason that She refers to Vietnam as "Au Lac" and Taiwan as "Formosa." Au Lac is the ancient name of Vietnam and means "happiness." And the name Formosa, meaning "beautiful," reflects more completely the beauty of the island and its people. Master feels that using these names brings spiritual elevation and luck to the land and its inhabitants.

The Village of Love
Amoura

Surrounded by ancient town and old forest, Amoura is around 220,000 m^2 with a population of 5/6 human (the scale tipped depends on "Tourism"), 10 dogs, some pet birds and teeming wild life.

Duck Avenue

Village's Park

It has a lake, half the size of the village. And most of the wild here depend on it for survival. The swans, the geese, ducks, coots, squirrels, beavers, rabbits, tortoises, rats, frogs and of course fishes, are those who take up residence around or in the lake.

A Villager's Residence

Fauna and Flora
of the Village

The deer and others like herons, owls, seagulls are non-residents, but come often and are always welcomed.

Stairway to a Residence

Others like squirrels, rabbits, birds of all kinds, and even a pair of young pigs prefer the woods surrounding the village. This village again is surrounded by an abundance of woods, extending miles all around, a favorite place for horse riding.

A Villager's Residence

Wild Beauty of Amoura

Most of the weekends, you can see riders and their horses stamping the ground with their footprints. And visitors also come here to take a fresh breath of air and bathe in nature's kindness.

The village is also belted with a long, deep and wide canal on one side and the beautiful river on the other. The scenery here is perfect. It's only befitting that beautiful and noble beings reside in this restful abode.

Red Garage
"Green" Parking

Camping in Amoura

11

When Autumn begins its visit in Amoura

We are going to meet them here, one group at a time.

Have fun!

Swanie Island in the famous Lake of Amoura!
(All residents know it!)

After a long winter (winter is always long!) Spring is suddenly here. Buddings seem to appear overnight. Surprise.

The lake also seems greener; the reflection of a tree-lined shore dyes its water emerald fresh and cool like a soothing dream, but one we can touch and feel with real mortal senses.

Spring at the lake

The gulls and the sunset
On the lake of Amoura

15

Some species of animals have individual names; Some don't.

16

Flowers and bushes promise a new natural harvest very soon to come. The birds do not frequent the feeder from the lady any more.

They have more abundance from Lady Nature and lots of exciting activities, tasting new berries, meeting friends and mates…

Life is lonely here?

It seems this way to the "blue" heron, too.

Looking for love?

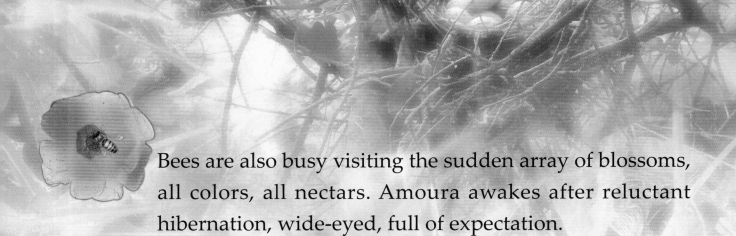

Bees are also busy visiting the sudden array of blossoms, all colors, all nectars. Amoura awakes after reluctant hibernation, wide-eyed, full of expectation.

And a lonesome Goose!

And to this single blue one! Life seems lonely also.

Not really
(Already)
We see!

Life in the village is anything but lonely. Four times a day, one can see an army of dogs rushing out from the main village residence, running around, barking at anything that moves (or not moves, depends on mood).

And one can hear a chorus of birds from inside their play pen, echoing the dogs. It can be quite deafening; lucky the place is big and the woods absorb somewhat the noise!

The Adventurous Team
Lady of the Village

This lady is one of the residents in Amoura.
She's quite busy exploring the surroundings and doing "Great"
works such as feeding the Ducks and Co.

   She seems serious about the job and loves doing it…

Question: Can a one-member group be called a team?
Answer: Yes! She & her boat.

The Ducks
Simple and Friendly Ones

... And most of the time she is "invisible" to outsiders, except if one happens to be a duck or a swan etc... Then one can expect a regular visit from her.

Meet the "Duck of Reedlington..."

… She often frequents lovely corners of Amoura such as Duck District, Swan Town, Frog Colony, Coot Settlement, etc…

She owns a "restaurant" at the far end of the village where customers flock in queue for the delicious menu. It opens for lunch and dinner, and anytime in between!…

... And the Duckess of Lilidale.

Lonely who?
Together we are cool

Duck's Resort in Amoura

And we have neighbors.
Guess who?

Yeah!
A goose

34

The soft ground is also our house.

Simple life is ours

36

This is another "lonesome" blue heron (Yes! Oh maybe he is blue.)

He (or she?) often rests on this exclusive spot reserved for bachelor herons – No one saw any other that landed there, ever.

Well, she (or he?) enjoys being in the sunshine nook. The sun rays stay there till late in the evening.

Very elusive – for a bachelor, you should be more sociable to chance a partner, methinks!

Bachelor nook

Like these two, for example, one can take as many close-ups as one likes. They come knocking at the main residence for food - sometimes 3-4 times a day.

They eat from your hands almost.

"Love is looking in the same direction"

The male is very attentive and protective of his mate.

If she's eating, he always stands guard – and if she runs to drink water, he'd run after her.

Don't worry, he eats sometimes – (witnessed).

Feeling fine
-- Anytime. --

41

Ducky's hang-out "Pub"

"Coming up!"

When she's resting next to the food after eating, or sleeping near-by, he'd come grab a few quick bites!

There's another guy chasing after her, and she's not keen on befriending that other one, so they are both very vigilant. Especially he, always on guard to protect his beloved.

So touching to observe such gentlemanerism.

"Ah! This is much better !
Even if you just sleep
by my side, we're together."

As these pages unfold before your eyes, autumn is already making its way through the village, weaving a golden blanket to keep the earth warm for coming winter.

- Foliage saying good-bye -

Flowers are donning their mature colors.

      Something is going,

      Something is coming.

The last flowers from summer still trying to array their glory, ignoring the call of time!

Even humans do the same here.

All sojourn contentedly

As if life in the physical...

... Is eternity.

Message from the sunset:
It is nice even to part
So there is joy of reunion.
    Something is withering,
    Something is growing.

Surprise!
Autumn bloomer.

The tranquil lake
Offers only solace,
A silent charm.
Always beautiful
Always calm.

Within this calmness
Life thrives in abundance
    The trees will be full and lush
    The littles will grow strong.

Something is blooming…
Something is thriving…

"This way my loves:
The bridge is way a-tall
To 'restaurant' we'll go."

"In God's Grace you will grow."

She has become a big mama
Protective and responsible
Takes care of her young at all cost
Finding food and shelter
Who is her teacher?!

She knows when to advance
When to run to the bush.
She knows when the golf cart comes
The lady will bring food.
So she'd gather all her children
Near the shore as usual
Eyes sparkling
Tail wagging!

But Mommy duck also taught little ones to be self-reliant –
hence they nib on green mosses that grow around the shores or
at shallow bottom lake sides. Seeing them happily munching
water weeds on dock poles or reeds, the lady was so moved:

Oh, how undemanding
the life they choose!

She doesn't take a morsel
All saved for her youngsters!
Guarding while they feed
Lest may be danger!

Oh! The love of a mother.
What else can one say!
Only the heart feels sympathy
And the eyes feel moist!

Watchful Guard

And so, day by day,
The siblings grow big and bigger.
Same devotion and love
From mother.

It is safer behind tall reeds
Near the shore.
Any little threat
Mother hurries them here.

Still, the brave mom
Teaches them to swim across
When the time has come
To learn about courage.

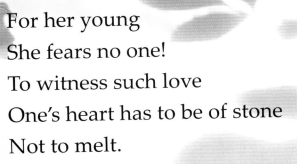

For her young
She fears no one!
To witness such love
One's heart has to be of stone
Not to melt.
    Sometimes the lady
        Feels overwhelmed with love
          For these wild creatures
           She just wished she could
            Them in her bosom to gather
             To hug and to caress them
              To show them the love in her.

Do you feel the strength of love,
    Do you see the awesome courage
        The true beauty in this mother's eyes?

Some eat on land

Some do on water
Food tastes the same

Still all enjoy
From the "provider."

72

A guardian angel
in the form of this humble mom

Don't worry my dears
You can well take rest
Ma is always here
Watching over my precious.

- Tired?
- No..o!

Really growing… fast!

Sharing with the gull.
It's OK, too!

Living together

Guess who's here for dinner

Peaceful solution!

Yes! There is work also
At the village's "office"

A real proud mother
A hero.
Wrestling with Nature
Against all odds
Against all dangers

"I am always here
For you."

Single-handedly
Raising her babies!

Now we have others
Joining the party.
The Canadian geese!

We go, wherever…
    It's the same water.

How come this guy
Still… so lonely?

Told you!
(Should be more sociable)
Seriously!

Squirrels
Planters of the Field

Do squirrels have names?
Yes, for sure.
Surprised?
Me too!

This is a young female named Sy (See)
She is so flamboyant and lovely,

Has an NQ of 10%!
Big Goodness
For such a tiny princess.

This auburn squirrel is a regular customer "Chez elle."
He has grown too comfy and confident
   That he even ventured into the house
      If couldn't find food outside
His name is Fy (Fi).

Some nut!
What kind?

Or curls up under his portable blanket
And sleeps right there
In front of the kitchen
After filling himself with bread.
(It's on the house!)

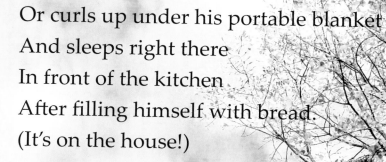

Bona Siesta!

… For the drink,
He must go to the lake,
Few yards away (poor thing!)

Sy is a young and beautiful red-head. When the first slice of bread was offered on the grass, she took it up close, turned it around and around to examine it attentively, so cute.

Then she tilted her head, looking again and again as if she has never seen this sort of nut before.

"What kind! So big, so square, so soft, yet so fragrant. Appetizing like Heaven!"

This is another one, male
    More mature, more "deep" in color and knowledge.

He is Zy (Zee).

94

This guy knows what's nut and what's not
No thing surprises him.
Done that.
Been there.
He explains to the younger ones
About life, how, why, what and where.
Quite a good elder!

Another frequent "Customer"!

Humans are my friends
And friend means *FOOD*
A Hem!...

My humble translation.
Accuracy?
Guaranteed!

Just check it out!

Your house is my house
(No doubt!)

Anyway I am free.

The planters of Amoura
Many nut trees are from them.

Come and go
As I please!

(I see!)

"We have something in common
We both like the bread from this home."

He loves nuts so much.

He looks like a nut!

Hut… Hut…

She eats fast
Like the way she runs.
Now you see it.
Now it's gone!

The proof of good cooking

Have a break
  Stroll around the lake
    Or visit the flowers…

          Or talk to the bamboos
            Amoura loves you!

103

The Horse
Good Neighbor

And preventer of the unfavorables.

The neighbor-horse does too.
(It helps if there's bread or apple!)

The Royal Canadian Geese

This is Fou
    Affectionately called Foo-Foo princess
      (By the lady)
      Such a love
        And beauty!

She originally came from neighboring lakes, but
somehow decided to stay in Amoura for a while.
    In winter, she does not move out.
    She must have felt OK here
    For she makes regular "appear."

Foo-Foo knows a good bakery when she tastes one!

This is another female geese
Her name is Sey-Sey.

At meal time, if the lady calls her name and she is near by
She would fly over to Amoura Lake,
     quacking all the way,
          To let the lady know: "Here is Sey-Sey."

She was all alone and young.
Maybe looking for a handsome,
The one that reflects her own,
Virtuous and gallant.

"I feel kinda lonely
Just I myself and me!"

This a male new-comer
Not so beloved by Sai Sai
He chases him whenever near by.
He is called Konay
A nice guy.

The old woman and the goose

There were two actually:
A young goose
And a past middle-age lady!
They understand each other
perfectly.

He often comes to the lady's house
For some food and a little love.
Sometime being chased by Sai Sai
(He chases anyone when he feels like
Just his sport to pass the time
Not hurting though.)

"It's not easy
Being dark
And different!
Is it the same
In the world of humans?"

She needs someone to share this
Beautiful "home" with.
Meanwhile, to be alone in quietude
Is also a blessing;
Though at times
It can feel lonesome!

Well!... Not any more!

Foo-Foo "introduced" Yeou, her beau, to the lady,
Who welcomed him heartily,
(the lady calls him Prince Yeou-Yeou)
He is so gorgeous and polite.
Whenever Foo takes a bath in the lake
He stands guard near by
On the small island or on the lake
At which their home they made.

Guarding Princess

And most of the time
    He also stands guard while she eats
Especially if they are on land
    At the lady's back yard park
        He would stand erect, vigilant
            On all sides, till she finished.

Then he might eat
If the situation is
Calm and favorable
No intruder, no threat
Or if food is still available,
Of course the lady makes sure
   To give ample portion for him
Then Foo-Foo would take turn now to guard.
While he eats, they don't "talk,"
   Just perfect telepathy.

They often come to the lady's house
Heads high and proud
Expecting a meal and love
They always get it!

After

Since the arrival of the little ones,
Foo-Foo has to constantly be on watch
Hardly has time to eat and rest.
  She became thinner but never
Let down her guard over
Her precious babies.
    Both of them actually:
      Yeou-Yeou also was doing
        His noble part of a parent
          Searching for food.
            And protecting the young.

Teaching them to forage
Teaching them all the "hows."
There're dangers in the wild
So, they always stay close.

Group with each other
Staying out of trouble…
– One never knows! –

Sometimes the father goes ahead
To check the path's OKness
For the safety of his family
He would lay down his life readily…

… Once a bigger "bully"
Swooped down upon them
The father did his best
To scare away the "baddy"
Though much smaller in size
He stood tall and tough
Stretching out his wings
In front of his kids
Covering his family
Till all little ones hurriedly
Followed Mum to safety.
Such a touching scene to see!

The lady was in tears…
So much worried!
They're in the water
She… on land!
Nothing she could do to prevent…
But she was so touched
Witnessing such courage and noble love!

The babies always stay close
And follow their mother
Never disobey or stray from her
Who is their teacher?...

They do not use any language
That the human knows of.
However, they understand each other
Perhaps more than humans do!
Strange! Don't you think so?

They are not talking
Yet there's perfect… "Sync!"

Harvest in Amoura

They are growing… and growing…
Now you can hardly tell
Who is the mother
Who is the sibling!

And the "colony" grows larger
Since it began summer.

Ah! Look at that, eh!
How lovely they are
God made them perfect!
Woa!

The meeting "club"
　　Of young goslings

And the lady is very happy
    To see them big, well and plenty
        Very very happy is she.
She welcomes them all
    With food and love, tenderly.

So beautiful is he!
Never seen one like this before
Has a name though:
"Or" !

He is so colorful! And so friendly

And not afraid of the lady
Comes quite near for bread!

He's adopted and loved,
  this "little Egyptian"

By these protective geese "parents"!

They always surround him
as if he's their most precious.

Yesterday - Life

Today - Demise

Simple charm in Amoura

Coots
The Shy Hermits

The Beginning of Courtship
Of Co and Ju

153

The Bridge Restaurant

A Beaver and a Coot
Racing for food
Odd combination
Same destination

154

Now u see me

A Master diver
Coots can stay long under
A similar size as pigeon
They're in the family of moor-hen.

Now u don't

On a tour of food supply
The lady discovered this nest.
　　Mom and Dad out for lunch
While this photo was taken.
She had to climb the tree and be quick
Before the parents are back.

　　Spring comes not only with flowers
　　But also lots of gifts to offer
　　Life blossoms anew…
　　After the long winter.

* A coot on her nest

The coots are much more of a hermit
Than the swans, geese or ducks.
They are also much smaller
Mostly they only come near
If other water-fowls are there.

      They would wait otherwise
      Till the human is out of sight
      Any slightest movement from the feeder
      They would take flight!

But there's one couple
Who come running when the lady is near
And partake of the food
That she daily thrice offers.

Even if one or both are hatching
On their nest at that moment
Mind you, only for food
Not to get too close, Eh!

The sign reads:
"Will be back after lunch"

The youngest sits and waits
The rest went with Mom & Dad away

The lady placed a little bread here
In case Mom couldn't find
Any food near.

There is still one more to come.
The mother is patient
The lady is "in waiting."

The parents keep coming and going
They never abandon the nest
But there are other offspring
That they must take care of.

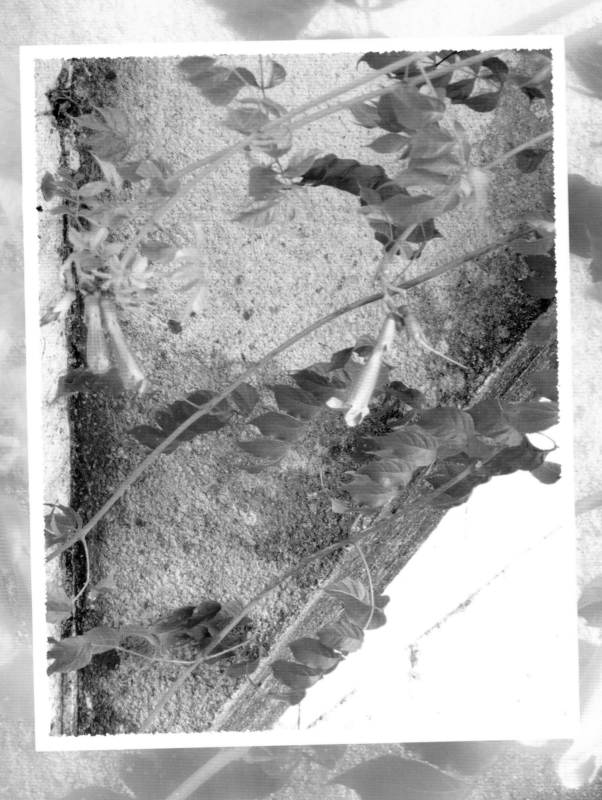

See the famous large feet
for swimming great is?

This little one kept going in the wrong direction
So the lady has to go on a "rescue mission."
She swooped it on to her boat
Carried it back to the parent's abode.

"It's comfortable here
I don't want to stir."

"I am not your mother

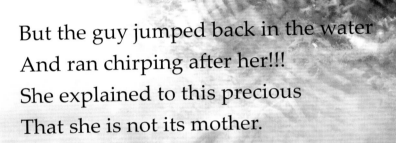

But the guy jumped back in the water
And ran chirping after her!!!
She explained to this precious
That she is not its mother.

Wanting to follow "Her."

"Hey, I do appreciate your love
But please go back to your flock
Mom and Dad will be worrying
If you go a-missing!"

Then, another nest here
My dear!
What a "Wonder-full" world!

Oblivious to the world

Song of the spring

And another nest after
Are they hatching forever!

They are here already
Only this latest one is not
in a hurry.

n any case
Such a work of love
And artistic design
Who is their guide?

"I like you
But do not come close"

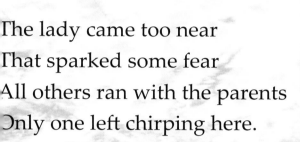

The lady came too near
That sparked some fear
All others ran with the parents
Only one left chirping here.

Though reclusive and maybe afraid
of human - who wouldn't, eh? –
The Mom and Dad kept coming near
To protect the little: Love is greater than fear!

The lady was in tears.
"I am so… sorry
I'd never hurt you
I'll leave right now!"

"…Just wanna feed you
Next time…
I won't come so close."

Panicked Mom and Dad
Going back and forth…
Hiding away the older ones
Trying to protect this little young

Who taught them all
this concern?

Raising a family

Dad, Mom and the cooties
Enjoying bread from the lady

This is long after they're hatched
The lady has regained their trust
Otherwise they'd hide near the shore
And parents take turns to carry food there.
And the "journey" could be long
Like from this shore to the other!

The lady wishes she could just fly
Here, there, to bring them the supplies!
Seeing coot Mama swam such a long distance
Carrying each morsel to her children
The lady's heart feels such tender love
Such an indescribable sentiment!

They would nip a piece in their beak
And swim away to feed their kids
It is a heartwarming scene to behold
In love they're nourished
And in love they grow!

- Who instructed them so?

We are also a united flock.

The building
     Of a "Bridge Restaurant"
It took one woman, two men
Some cables, some fence
Three days, no cement
The lady was the "engineer"
The two men were good helping hands

The access to Swanie Island
The white "dot" above is
    a hatching swan

Great Crested Grebe
The Reclusive Diver

The shade of time

This is as good as it gets
The photo is already the best
Anyway they are
Similar size as ducks,
A little more slender.
(Just enjoy the Autumn lake color!)

This water beauty never came
Close enough for a better vision.
Bread or stuffs never tempted him
They just love to dive and swim.

If you feel it's disappointing
Please stop further looking.
The worse photos are coming!

Well, it's better than nothing
At least, to show their existence.
With binoculars, they are fascinating!

Deer Road

The signature of Autumn

Yeah! I am asking for the same answer:
No no no! It's not a hammer,
It's a great crested grebe

It's a bird!
If you don't believe,
Go nearer and see
      Ha... Ha!

Oh! He ran away even further.
Will try to get a better picture.
(Serious!) - OK?

Great Crested Grebe (à la Ching Hai!)
Through binoculars.

Thanks to the computer – he has "grown" bigger.

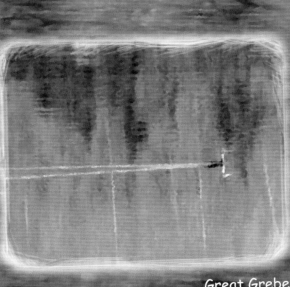

Great Grebe

Greater Grebe?

    (Ha ha! No, it's the same guy.)

Great Crested Grebe (à la Ching Hai!)
Looked through binoculars

(In case) you don't like the picture of the other guy!
Maybe this is his buddy!

Glorious summer
Saying it with flowers

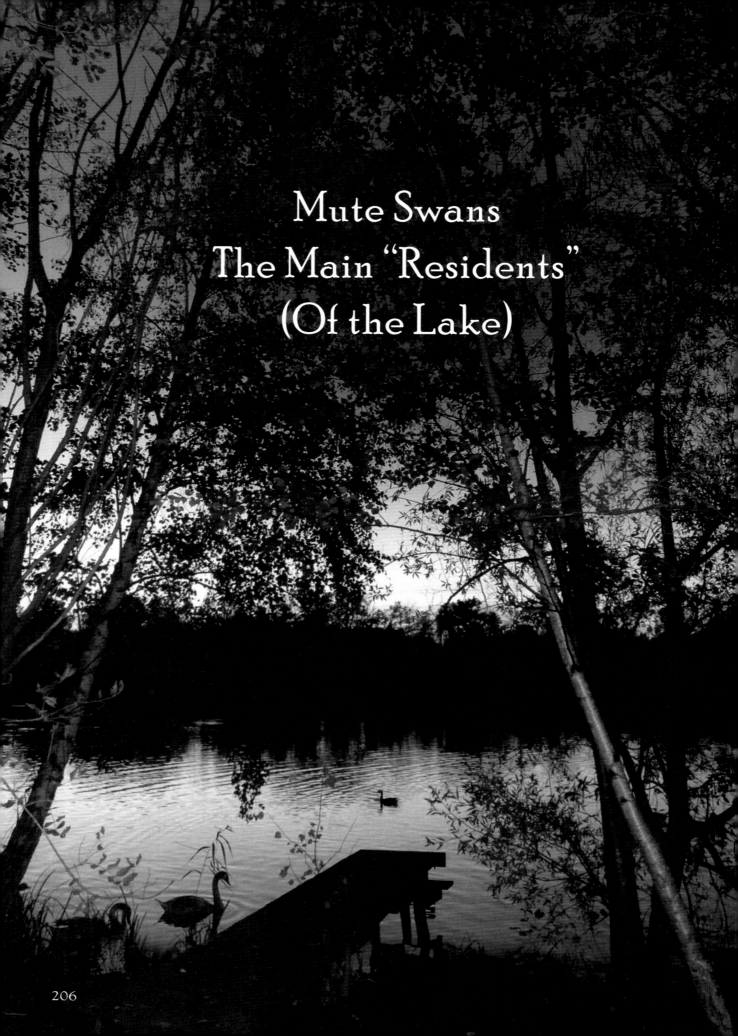

Mute Swans
The Main "Residents"
(Of the Lake)

Gina & Moruwey

In the beginning was the (S)… wan
Beautiful, young and lonesome
Visiting an old lady's home.
Gina is her name.

208

We are friends

Gina and the lady

Gina has a daughter swanie
Said her name is Moruwey
(Don't ask me!)
Who loves to be among gulls.
They get on so well!

Who can blame you
Peace and quiet, huh!

Look at the two of them
Lovely beyond description!
– Born friendly and tame –

The threesome friends
Sharing simple lunch.
Having nice "Conversation."

But they moved away
When the spring arrived
Ah, reunion and depart
So, it's life.

By the way,
"How old is old?"

"We do not have to use verbal language. We communicate in silence. We need not talk about love, harmony and peace. We live in them."

Pitu

Pitu & Sai

After a short while
There came this beauty.
She is tender young and lovely
Loves to befriend the lady.

"This is "PeeToo"
(Written Pitu)
She came from far away
Finland is home – she says –

Vis à vis?

Lonesome Beauty

She enjoys herself greatly
On the Amoura water
Feeling so… care free.

Pitu in her natural habitat
Gloriously beautiful
And smart

223

Pitu enjoys her home
Seems to love being alone.

Not for long

Here comes "The one."
His name is Sai:
Saying from India

Handsome, tough and strong
Macho 100%.

Crowded Restaurant
- Famous food!-
(Whole-meal bread and lettuce are good)

228

The Future
More Somes

And the two-some of them
Produce some more "somes."
Here's Pitu hatching…
Concerned about her
The lady brought food and care!

She rows for daily visit

Petit – Princess Island

For a diligent, among the best Moms
The distance is never too long.

"I'll take care of your family
Like I did a long time ago.
Nice to see you again good friend
How many there under your wings?"

So…o…Many.
I'm proud of you
Dear loved Pitu!

234

One on one.
(One in a nest
One in the tent)

"It's thoughtful to bring me some drink
But I'll get water from the abundance,
What do you think?... Thanks!"

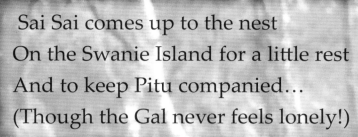

Sai Sai comes up to the nest
On the Swanie Island for a little rest
And to keep Pitu companied…
(Though the Gal never feels lonely!)

237

Pitu is turning the hatchlings
Sai Sai is nearby guarding.

… And to check on mother and dears
Most of the time he stands guard on water.
(… Do not venture near here,
Sai can really teach you fear!)

The proud owner of Bridge Restaurant

The "communication" begins
Between Ma and future siblings

Pitu would pluck her silky feathers
To inlay the nest softer
Day and night, rain or shine
She protects her nestlings as her life.

The lady brings daily supply
Of Pitu's favorite and for Sai.
They love soft bread, lettuce and spinach.

Pitu in her nest and dining room.

The lady supplies all that they need
She even camped next door to them
(Not a good idea, don't try at home!)

The Swans didn't mind she came and went
They were used to her by then.
Still, it's best to stay away
They are fiercely protective of their family!

One day the lady used a stick of wood
Tried to remove something from their nest
Because it seemed to pierce the body of Pitu
But she went berserk, called Sai to Shoo
He flew to her immediately.
Advancing with pumped up giant body
With deliberate threatening gesture and Hissing

This is the "Fence connection"
That she uses to get to the island
It's quicker and also much safer
(Sometimes Sai doesn't allow the boat to enter!)

Cornering and almost pushed the lady down.
But she said "I am good, I am good.
I only wanted to help Pitu
The stick from her neck to remove
I am good to you!"
He calmed down instantly
And went back down to the water! Whewph…!

Later, the lady moved her tent
Near to the bridge, on higher elevation.
Just to watch over the swans
And wait for the blossoming of the little ones!

The lady's quarters
On Swanie Island.

The Moresomes

Again: "Can one person be called a team?"
– Who cares!

Here they are, oh dear!
Who makes them so adorable?
The lady was beyond happy
Tending to them like her babies.

We are all waiting
But this one doesn't like coming
Oh well. If it's willing not
Maybe it feels better in Heaven!

The lady abandoned her tent
Not wanting to disturb them
Respecting their privacy
She camped in another place nearby.

Now you see them

Now you don't

Before going on exploration
Listen well to the good guidance.

First-time outing on water
With Papa.

It's not difficult to know
Who's Sai and who is Pitu
Sai has a bigger body and black feet.
Pitu's more slender, light "paws," and chic.

261

Pitu is also the more noble of the two
Elegant, gentle and beautiful.
There is something about her, inborn
That commands respect and admiration.

Trusting Ma
in unknown waters.

Home sweet home.

Only fifteen or so days old
They already can travel
Paying the old lady a grateful visit
She's waiting happily
For her extended family.

When the training get tough
When the wind is too rough
There's good transportation
Quick, comfy and convenient.

Sai is chewing the food to bits:
Easier for the kids to eat.

The siblings can eat at all times
Taking very short naps
During hatching time and after even
One hardly sees the parents resting!

It was still very cold in mid-spring
At night temp drops to plus 5-6
Pitu sat on duty and rarely moved.
Sai never slept all night through
He was constantly vigilant – deep in the icy water.
The lady camped near and fed Sai-Sai
He came often for a quick bite.
How did Pitu survive so long
Who helps her stay healthy and strong?
Who keeps Sai Sai through the night warm?

Even after the babies are hatched
Pitu hardly eats nor sleeps much!
Her weight came low
Her feathers thinning
She plucked them to quilt their nest
Now she has only half her wings!
Seeing thus the lady kept crying

Carpeted the ground
That your tender feet walk!
Know that you are
Loved!

1/2 winged

Waiting for the wings to return.

Has only 1/2 wings

She cannot fly nor does want to
Her life is bound with the littles

The lady's heart feeling some pain
Seeing Pitu's body thus waned
The lady keeps singing her name, coaxes her to eat
Sometimes succeeds, most often nicht!

Thus day by day the littlings grow
So does the lady's love for them and Pitu
She loves Sai also, but it's different.
She feels more sympathy for mother swan.

274

Pitu was always watchful over her precious. Sometimes chasing fishes away, sometimes beavers or any intruder that might come too near. Well, the swanlings are still very fragile and small, who could blame her?

The lady keeps trying to convince Pitu to eat something:

"Come on Pitu, please eat so that you stay strong and healthy, so that you can take care of your babies, please Pitu, please! It hurts me to see you so thin and having so little rest. Please eat."

Then she broke the whole meal bread into chew sizes, threw them next to Pitu; Pitu would eat a little, but then too distracted by other "intruder" – or just busy watching in all directions, making sure her babies are safe.

One just has to witness it to feel what the lady feels for Pitu. Words fail to express when it comes to sympathy and love!

But Sai is also very diligent and smart.
He does more than his share for his children.
No one knows how he went sleepless
Soaked in cold water during hatching
He rarely went ashore, relentlessly guarding.

His eyes penetrate the whole lake
He left no chance, he missed nothing.
One time the lady's boat was too near
He circled around to tell us "Disappear!"
He was polite at first
But when we persisted, he went berserk
Becoming war-like
Till we got it and "fly."

Sai must have been very tired
He snores!

279

Only after the kids grow bigger
Seem less prone to predators and danger
That they take turns to cool their heads
Life in the wild (must be lots of stress)!

280

The secret hide-out

On this island
Lots of residents
Swans, ducks, coots, rats, beavers…
All sizes, all shapes and all colors

Growing together as community
Here is ducks' and swans' colony.

The "Swan connection"

Guarding treasures
On the lady's back yard
On their island or on water
On familiar ground
On strange land…

Or wherever…
One never knows!
They are too fragile and little.
If the kids like it here
The parents would stand guard forever!

You can tell who's Papa?
Right, the black feeter
And he's always in alert poised
Big and scarier!
– To ward off any intruder –
Think twice before you go near
        (Don't ever)

Leave the rest…
    … for the geese?

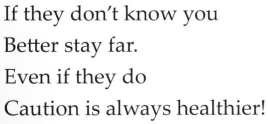

If they don't know you
Better stay far.
Even if they do
Caution is always healthier!
    For their babies, they'd act in frenzy!
      Don't even try.

Even if their feeding abounds
The parents always dig some plant out
To teach their kids all about survival
All the arts of know-how.

Though tough to strangers,
To their kids, extremely tender.
Their love and sacrifice
Will bring tears to your eyes.

And although Sai is protective to his kids
He still remembers the lady's kindness
Mostly he is very polite to her
Always flies to where she is
Or whenever she calls.
(If he happens to be without the kids)
When she arrives to feed
They'd all come around and wagging tails
Not kidding, it's real!
(The ducks and their kids do the same though.)

One time the lady was so upset
Seeing little coots being harassed
She talked to Sai of how she felt
Tears in her eyes as sadness welled

He looked at her and flew straight to the water
Chasing away that "bad" oppressor
Came back and stood around the lady
Puffing his wings and held his head proudly
But with sympathetic gestures.
So astonished was she
There was a silent telepathy
Hard to explain
But she would assure you
That Sai understood
Every single thing she said
In English, eh!

If you know a wild
Try it yourself!
Don't be surprised
At their rapport,
Humans are the ones,
Who know not a lot!

For now, they are the most devoted
Loving parents and loyal guardians
Touching the hearts of any-one!

See how the parents stand by
Watching them eat?
Their most favorite!
They hardly ever touch any.
But just feed themselves lake weeds!

The children are on the grow
It seems they can always eat!
The lady keeps giving,
The kids keep munching.
They feed every two, three hours
All day and all night.
They don't just feed on lettuce & bread,
Sai and Pitu teach them the wild diet.
It's good for them to learn independence.
The lady knows when to give what and when none.

When the kids were still small
Sai always chewed their food to little
Or gestured to them, "Here, take it"
One can observe all their "speech."

Rush hour

Near the royal Bridge Restaurant

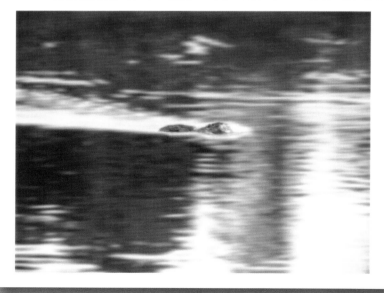

Hi!
Heavenly PaMa of Mine!

We are near
Come on dears.
The lady is waiting
With food and luving.

Swan Boulevard.

They always lie down
On her yard to eat
Not shy, not ashamed, not afraid.
They love fresh lettuce
She loves to feed!

Lunch chez lady's palace
Crispy lettuce and wholesome bread
After such long and tired swimming
It's so good to relax and enjoying.

Really Growing

See what I mean?

In the water

They all look smaller

But when on land

They're almost big as mother!

But still

They stick close to her

And always show obedience

"Mother knows best" – they think.

Last piece of lettuce
Still tastes delicious!

310

They share every thing
Never trifle or competing
Such peace and harmony!
Wishing it on all beings.

At such tender age
Already knows sailing
He uses only one paddle here
To balance stable "standing."

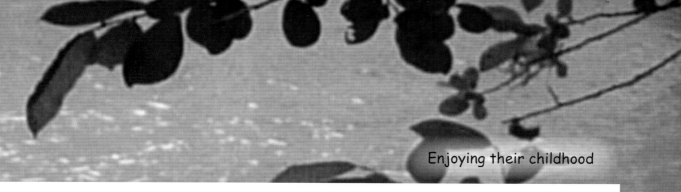

Sometime they frolic
In the lake water
Like standing erect on it
Or diving deep down under
Taking a dip and another dip
Or grooming their silky pluffy feathers.

Who are you,
that comes and goes?

How come the swans
Look so like the trees!
Who made their differences,
Who made their similarities?

The lady hears
The lady sees:
The swans do snore
Like "every" body!

It must be taxing
Watching every noise
Hearing every shade
Twenty four vingt-quatre.
But Sai and Pitu
Carry out with gladness
Like all parents do.
We salute you
We salute the great love in all.

Wild Serenity

Under the "great protection"
Every place seems like Heaven.

Feels like "Chez moi" *

* at home

Feeling safe
Even the parents
Can afford to sleep!
Letting off guard.
(Only at their place
And the lady's yard)

Growing fast…
And strong!

Getting a little whiter

... Wandering all over the land

Mostly the length and breadth of the lake
Or the "restaurant" at the bridge
Or to the lady's house.
She leaves food at various places
For them to find out (like natural)
If not, they would come knocking
First only Sai or both go checking
If the lady is there, they'd hiss
To signal them to come, the kids.

They'd always sit there and wait
Ever so quiet and polite.
Only Sai "puffs up" a little
Seeing his reflection as another guy
He'd walk back and forth, to and fro
Ready to defend against whom-so-ever

Sai goes first to clear the way
And to check if the food's ready.
When he sees the sign of bread
He'd go back to bring the family.

The thing is that they all will part
When the time comes as the kids grow up
Like nothing has ever happened.
Such unconditional love and detachment!

The beauty
Is already
Evident…

White feathers
Hidden under wings!

Getting whiter!

Getting flowery

Learning to be independent
And obedient is the beginning
Of good leadership

"Do what I tell you
And do what I do"

338

The "unsocial" heron
Still blue and still alone!
He is just a tourist and unknown.

Teeming with friendly society

339

I'll be like Mumy

But I am already pretty!

342

See the white feathers
Round my wings and under?

And I can fly
Far and wide!

We are big things!
We are already flying
Though it's still short distance
We can feel our powerful wings!
We are three and half months old.
And we still grow!
Over the trees and in mid-air
Our vision expands, everywhere.

Already as big as Mama!

Growing "too big" and beautiful
For the poor camera

Like Father

Like child.

Morning Calm

Very early morning, even the sun did not want to wake up yet; a veil of fog is spread over the whole lake and most of its surroundings, but the winged residents and "not" are already on their way for breakfast.

It must have been very cold in the night, and they'd have felt the need to replenish their energy, especially the young ones who need to be fed often.

In their early days, their parents took the swanlings out to feed every few hours, day & night.

Doesn't that sound familiar?

Yeah! To the human counterparts.

Doing fine, kid!
You are the eldest
It's OK to take the lead
Take care of yourself
And each other
When soon you'll grow much older.

Thank to God, the greatest designer
Who sends decoration for the lady's front yard
All the residents in the village
Enjoy these delicate beauties so much!

It's Pitu who teaches
The art of flying to the kids
First a short distance only
Then the lake's entirety.

Sai has in turn lost half
The feathers of his wings
Perhaps he's molting
Perhaps he plucked them off
To soften the cold ground of their nest.

Or perhaps he was tired
Taking care of family and on guard
Day and night for many months
It's taxing, even if he's strong.
But that doesn't make him weak
He still scares off the geese
If they ever dare to venture
Somewhere near his dear treasures.

Though he doesn't mind
For his kids to sacrifice.
It must be frustrating now
Always lagging behind!

Sai, the great!
Now, only half-winged
Still fast sailing
Still beautiful
Still magnificent.
  Still can scare away
  Any intruding.

358

Sai only half winged
Still diligent
Still an excellent guardian

There are hundreds of geese together, but they never
compete for food - Never fight back with "big" swans,
always well behaved, gentle and peaceful

Although Sai sometimes shoos away the biggies,
he is very gentle with 'smallings' like sea gulls,
calling them to share food.

And whenever the lady is near, he digs up
plants from the lake bottom to offer to her!

Share with Seagull

Tough Sai Sai, Oh!
Eating without much of the usual gusto.
When you're lonely,
No!

Lonely for a day
Sai without Pitu and kids
They have flown far away
And his wings have not grown back yet!

Night view of the moon light
While waiting for the swanlings
And Pitu to return from their
first long-range-flight

Little Marvel
Precious Gardener

I enjoy simple lunch
Supplied by the Providence
I also prune the shrub
Keep a nice and neat garden.

She takes life leisurely
  He takes time to journey
She enjoys her breakfast
  Fresh, nutri-full and ready…

Tiny resident
  Groomer of the garden
    God loves him so much
      Hes made him radiant!

* Precious life
Beautiful color
Who creates her design
So precise and bright!

I may be tiny
  But to an ant…

… I am a biggy!

371

Ain't I beautiful!

God always gives flowers
To the lady in spring and summer.

Beavers
The Constructors

Meet Nu the beaver
The dam builder
Proud and loving Dad
Bridge Restaurant's regular customer.

Undercover guest
Enjoying the bread

Small creature
Big character
A 10 NQ-er

And meet lady beaver

Quiet and timid Zu

She would eventually come near

After a while knowing you.

Of course not rushing like Nu

She is a graceful lady though.

The only son: So
From the beaver couple

Yeh! come meet the third party So
That you may watch and adore.
His parents told him not to fear
So he comes when the lady's near.
Of course the food is a helping factor!
He is so cute and smart little doll.

See how Nu holds the bread in his hands
Eating calmly like a gentle man
But he chews quite fast and eats a lot
(He needs it after much construction work.)

Isn't he beautiful?

|||||||||||||||||||

He's no longer afraid of any human
The first to rush here to Bridge Restaurant
Then goes from one slice of bread to another
Precise, never hesitates or wavers.

Zu is still shy and reserved
Stays a little distance and not eating that much!
Zu is a bit smaller.
And her face is round and pinkier.

See the difference between the two
Zu stays little far way, and so close is Nu
But they are both so… cool!

Beaver
The ten percenter
10% NQ!

Miss Beaver "Do"
Pronounced "Du"

One is grateful feeling love here
The tiny blossoms bring God's love near.
On the garden's slender grass blades
A magnificent message of grace…

Fish
The Mysterious

Camping with spider's family!

Fish & bread

The fishes also love bread
They always join in at the fest
Here they come to enjoy their dinner
Glad not to be on a lunch table!

Here is another fish who came to the party
We celebrate abundance and life every day
The residents on and off the lake love it
All joyfully partake of the treats
God's love is upon all who know Hiers name
Glorious praise to The ONE in the entire creation!

The mysterious "Figure"
With three mysterious colors!

Mysterious creatures!
Maybe a monster?
No, no, they are just fishes
Coming up for dinner.

The trace of time

Gulls
The Sociable Tourists
Sharing And Caring...

The gull tourists
    Carrying food in their beaks.
        Whenever the Bridge Restaurant opens
        They call each other to come at once
            All share together with ducks and swans...
            They never eat alone.

These are the "Foreign tourists"
With strange tales from west to east.

They are happy to know this land
That has festival every day - no end.

"Where we came from, there's 'no free lunch'
But over here they give you food and drink
We love it much, we stay longer
Here we have every thing that we wish for."

The glory of wild grass!
Who makes them thus?

Garden Birds
The Joy Bringers
Some Say Even Luck!

Yoo hoo!

These are beautiful birds
That became the regulars
If there's no food on the grass
They would come knocking on the glass!...

Where go?

Let me go and see
If I can talk to the lady
The food she gave is much nicer than this
I'll be back – real quick

The lady always comes to feed them.
They became almost like friends
There's not a word spoken between them
Just a love that's simple and untamed.

Meanwhile I eat what's here!

Let's go over there
Bread is scattered every where!...
    We don't want to eat this stuff
    I'll show you what real food is,
    Hurry up!

You better be right!
I'd also like to try.

Wild nutrients!

Oh this guy is really fast
There's no one when I was here last.

Anyway, we all can share
There's enough under the lady's care.

There, there!
Pick it up
And try the stuff.
Don't worry
It's good
Guaranteed!

Ah! Ah! Wait for me my dear
But it is even safe to eat right here!

The Magnolia
On the lady's back yard

Some Other Kinds of Residents

There's always some activities with some residents in the village. Chasing your own shadows or chasing your tails are some. Or just hanging around, hanging onto the wall, barking at random... are favorite pass-times of quite a few co-inhabitants.

Others prefer hanging on the ceiling, quacking at themselves or talking to his/her own tail, or toys in some cases.

Oh they do watch TV, video too, like every one else heh!

Birds' play pen

Some dog's home!!!

Guess whose home!

There's always
some special program
in the village
with the residents.

(The guy is in love
Can you see?)

420

Like… hanging on the wall.

Or… hanging around

Some kind of "body" guard?

No! A guarded body.

BROKEN
GLASS
B. CAREFUL

422

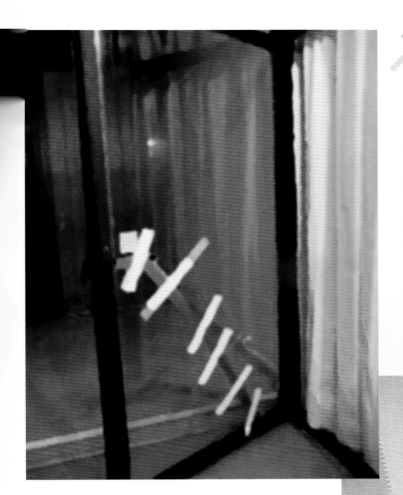

When you have clumsy
2-legged and big 4 leggy
as residents in a house
What will be the result?

(Answer:
Broken glass!!!)

BROKEN
GLASS
B. CAREFUL!
♡

The village road
And some "invisible" residents

Sweet home of the lady

425

Some of the residents

Are "ascetic"! = sleeping on the bare floor!

(only in…summer)

Pillow fight, anyone?

Oh well!
I'll just use it for myself

Waiting for the swans
Or ducks, or squirrels
Or birds…
Or whatever

Other kinds of residents
(Actually, they're similar)

428

The leisured "activities"

Me like you
Me love the cool floor, too.

Training
for action???

A relaxy resi

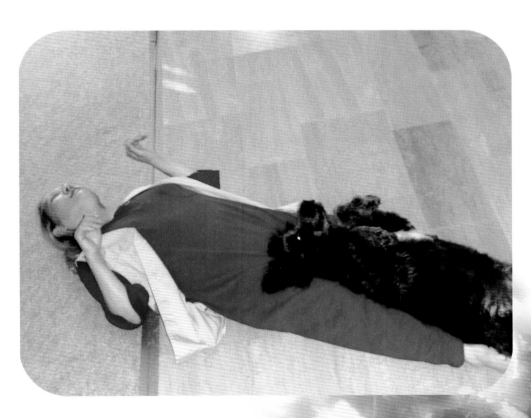

In Amoura Villy.

Golden girls of Amoura.

Self serving buffet.

The lady's "home bakes"
(She's behind the cakes!)

Pretend to be sleeping

Meditating?

Chatting to your own tail is
   a pass-time hobby

Hanging around
Hanging out

Hanging about
Hanging anyhow!

Chatting about things

Sweet home of the same lady

A visit by the fog, at the lady's home

The sovereignty of the fog

And the untamed garden

The Universal Connection

This pregnant goat (named "Bu") stumbled from the mountain slope into a ditch behind a fence. (She had not eaten anything for several days and became very weak.) The lady freed her, fed her and searched for the right caretaker to return her to her flock, as per Bu's request. She was so excited, trembling when she overheard the lady's phone conversation reading her tag number to the prospective "carer."

All the four-legged (dog) residents did not bark at her. (Well, only once at the first surprise encounter) They were so gentle around her as not to frighten the desperate goat all the while that she was in their "land." The lady was so proud of their good behavior! Praised them hugely!

After numerous phone calls to different places, her caretaker was found! She did not want to leave the lady's yard when her "carer" arrived. So the lady's assistants had to carry her to his van. She kept looking at the lady with loving eyes. It was not easy for her to part with Bu, though they had only short acquaintance. But Bu wanted to reunite with her love "Ro" - and she will be happier there!

Carer of Bu the Goat came to pick her up!

Good luck Bu!
The lady gave Bu's carer some money, making him promise to call a vet, take good care of Bu and her child. He did promise!

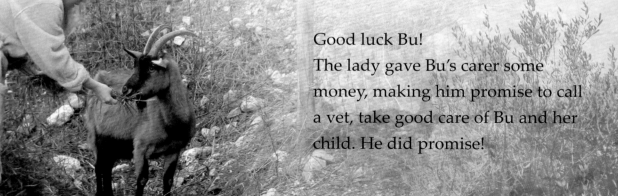

446

Bu out of the ditch waiting for her "carer"

The next afternoon, the vet called to tell us that Bu is OK, no serious injury. But she advised her carer to give her good rest, not moving long distance but stay in her shed with her flock. Bu had lost 3 kilos during the hungry days in the ditch! But she's OK otherwise! And Bu is going to have twin babies. (She did tell the lady that she's having "children.")

We called to thank the carer for letting us know through the vet about Bu's well being; although we had requested, but weren't sure that he would do so! And though Bu already informed the lady, she's so glad to know the confirmation physically.

The Spiritual Teachings by The Supreme Master Ching Hai

The Key of Immediate Enlightenment

A collection of The Supreme Master Ching Hai's lectures. Available in Aulacese (1-15), Chinese (1-10), English (1-5), French (1-2), Finnish (1), German (1-2), Hungarian (1), Indonesian (1-5), Japanese (1-4), Korean (1-11), Mongolian (1,6), Portuguese (1-2), Polish (1-2), Spanish (1-3), Swedish (1), Thai (1-6), and Tibetan (1).

The Key of Immediate Enlightenment – Questions and Answers

A collection of questions and answers from Master's lectures.
Available in Aulacese (1-4), Bulgarian, Chinese (1-3), Czech, English (1-2), French, German, Hungarian, Indonesian (1-3), Japanese, Korean (1-4), Portuguese, Polish, and Russian.

The Key of Immediate Enlightenment – Special Edition/Seven-Day Retreat

A collection of Master's lectures in1992 during a Seven-Day Retreat in San Di Mun, Formosa. Available in English and Aulacese.

The Key of Immediate Enlightenment – Special Edition/1993 World Lecture Tour

A six-volume collection of The Supreme Master Ching Hai's lectures during the 1993 World Lecture Tour. Available in English and Chinese.

Letters Between Master and Spiritual Practitioners

Available in Aulacese (1-2), Chinese (1-3), English (1), Spanish (1)

The Key of Immediate Enlightenment –My Wondrous Experiences with Master (1-2)

Available in Chinese and Aulacese.

Master Tells Stories

Available in Aulacese, Chinese, English, Japanese, Korean, Spanish, and Thai.

Of God and Humans – Insights from Bible Stories

Available in English and Chinese.

God Takes Care of Everything
Illustrated Tales of Wisdom from The Supreme Master Ching Hai

Aulacese, Chinese, English, French, Japanese, and Korean.

The Supreme Master Ching Hai's Enlightening Humor –
Your Halo Is Too Tight!

Available in Chinese and English.

Coloring Our Lives

A collection of quotes and spiritual teachings by Master. Available in Chinese and English.

Secrets to Effortless Spiritual Practice

Available in Chinese and English.

God's Direct Contact – The Way to Reach Peace

A collection of The Supreme Master Ching Hai's lectures during Her 1999 European Lecture Tour.
Available in English and Chinese.

I Have Come to Take You Home

Available in Arabic, Aulacese, Bulgarian, Czech, Chinese, English, French, German, Greek, Hungarian, Indonesian, Italian, Korean, Polish, Spanish, Turkish, Romanian, and Russian.

Living in the Golden Age series
The Realization of Health – Returning to the Natural and Righteous Way of Living

Collected excerpts from the lectures of Supreme Master Ching Hai.
Available in English and Chinese.

Aphorisms

Gems of eternal wisdom from Master.
Available in English/Chinese, Spanish/Portuguese, French/German, and Korean.

The Supreme Kitchen – International Vegetarian Cuisine

A collection of culinary delicacies from all parts of the world recommended by fellow practitioners.
Available in English/Chinese, Aulacese, and Japanese.

The Supreme Kitchen – Home Taste Selections

Recipes in a bilingual edition: English /Chinese.

One World... of Peace through Music

A collection of interviews and musical compositions from the 1998 benefit concert at the Shrine Auditorium in Los Angeles, California.
Trilingual edition: English/Aulacese/Chinese.

S.M. Celestial Clothes

Available in bilingual edition: English/Chinese.

The Collection of Art Creations by The Supreme Master Ching Hai – Painting Series

Through the painting of an artist, the artist's inner Self is revealed. You will be deeply touched by the intense affection, childlike innocence and motherly love of the liberated One.
Available in English and Chinese.

The Dogs in My Life (1-2)

This two-volume book set of 500 pages is a fabulous real-life set of doggy tales published by Master about Her canine companions.
Available in English and Chinese.

The Birds in My Life

In this beautifully illustrated picture-story book, Master Ching Hai shows us the secret to unlocking the animals' inner world.
Available in English and Chinese.

Poetry Collections by
The Supreme Master Ching Hai

Wu Tzu Poems
Available in Aulacese, Chinese and English.

Silent Tears
Available in English/German/French, English/Chinese, Aulacese, Spanish, Portuguese, Korean and Filipino.

The Dream of a Butterfly
Available in Aulacese, Chinese and English.

The Old Time
Available in Aulacese and English.

Pebbles and Gold
Available in Aulacese, Chinese and English.

The Lost Memories
Available in Aulacese, Chinese and English.

Traces of Previous Lives
Available in Aulacese, English and Chinese.

Traces of Previous Lives 1, 2, 3 (CD, Video, Audio tapes) Aulacese

A Path to Love Legends 1, 2, 3 (CD, Video, Audio tapes) Aulacese

Beyond the Realm of Time (CD, DVD) Aulacese

A Touch of Fragrance (CD) Aulacese

That and This Day (CD) Aulacese

Dream in the Night (CD, DVD) Aulacese

What the Hell! (CD) Aulacese

Please Keep Forever (CD) Aulacese

Songs & Compositions of The Supreme Master Ching Hai
(CD, DVD) English, Aulacese, Chinese

Song of Love
Supreme Master Ching Hai sings timeless songs in English and Aulacese
(CD, DVD) English, Aulacese

Jeweled Verses
(CD, DVD)
Song performance and poetry recitation in Aulacese by Supreme Master Ching Hai, written
by renowned Aulacese poets.

The Golden Lotus
 (CD, DVD)
We invite you to listen to the recital of Venerable Thich Man Giac's beautiful poetry, through
the melodious voice of Supreme Master Ching Hai, who also recited two of Her own poems,
"Golden Lotus" and "Sayonara".

Audio and Video Publications

Audio tapes, DVDs, music concerts DVD, CDs, MP3s and video tapes of The Supreme
Master Ching Hai's lectures and Music & Concert DVDs are available in Arabic, Armenian,
Aulacese, Bulgarian, Cantonese, Cambodia, Chinese, Croatian, Czech, Danish, Dutch,
English, Finnish, French, German, Greek, Hebrew, Hungarian, Indonesian, Italian, Japanese,
Korean, Malay, Mongolian, Nepali, Norwegian, Mandarin, Polish, Portuguese, Persian,
Russian, Romanian, Sinhalese, Slovenian, Spanish, Swedish, Thai, Turkish and Zulu.
Catalog will be sent upon request. All direct inquiries are welcome.
Please visit our bookshop's website to download our catalogue and summaries of the
contents of Master's latest publications:
http://www.smchbooks.com/ (in English and Chinese).
To order Master's publications,
please visit http://www.theCelestialShop.com to purchase online.
Or contact:
The Supreme Master Ching Hai International Association Publishing Co., Ltd., Taipei, Formosa
Tel: (886) 2-87873935 / Fax: (886) 2-87870873
E-mail: smchbooks@Godsdirectcontact.org
ROC Postal Remittance Account No.19259438 (for Formosa orders only)
Postal Account: : The Supreme Master Ching Hai International Association Publishing Co., Ltd.

Free Sample Booklet download
The Key of Immediate Enlightenment
(in 60 languages)
http://sb.godsdirectcontact.net/
http://www.direkter-kontakt-mit-gott.org/download/index.htm
http://www.Godsdirectcontact.org/sample/
http://www.Godsdirectcontact.us/com/sb/

How to Contact US

The Supreme Master Ching Hai International Association
P.O. Box 9, Hsihu Miaoli Hsien, Formosa (36899), R.O.C.
P.O.Box 730247, San Jose, CA 95173-0247, U.S.A.

Book Department
divine@Godsdirectcontact.org
Fax: 1-240-352-5613 / 886-949-883778
(You are welcome to join us in translating Master's books into other languages.)

The Supreme Master Ching Hai International Association Publishing Co., Ltd.
smchbooks@Godsdirectcontact.org
Tel: 886-2-87873935
Fax: 886-2-87870873
http://www.smchbooks.com

News Group
lovenews@Godsdirectcontact.org
Fax: 1-801-7409196 / 886-946-728475

Spiritual Information Desk
lovewish@Godsdirectcontact.org
Fax: 886-946-730699

A Journey through Aesthetic Realms TV Program Videotapes
TV@Godsdirectcontact.org
Fax: 1-413-751-0848 (USA)

S.M. Celestial Co., Ltd.
smcj@mail.sm-cj.com
Tel: 886-2-87910860
Fax: 886-2-87911216
http://www.sm-cj.com

Celestial Shop
http://www.theCelestialShop.com
http://www.edenrules.com

Quan Yin WWW Sites

God's direct contact—The Supreme Master Ching Hai International Association's global Internet:
http://www.Godsdirectcontact.org.tw/eng/links/links.htm

This portal provides a directory of links to Quan Yin Web sites in a variety of languages, as well as 24-hour access to Supreme Master Television. You may also download multilingual editions of *The Key of Immediate Enlightenment Sample Booklet*, or download or subscribe to *The Supreme Master Ching Hai News* available in eBook or printable format, or simply browse the sites' contents online.

Supreme Master Television
Info@SupremeMasterTV.com
Tel: 1-626-444-4385
Fax: 1-626-444-4386
http://www.suprememastertv.com/

Alternative Living

We Pray for You

Change Your Life
Change Your Heart
Change Your Diet

♥------♥

No more killing
Be healthy and loving

Save our Lives! We Love You

Examples of nutritious, life saving food:

Foods	Protein Concentration (Percentage by Weight)
Tofu (from soya)	16 %
Gluten (from flour)	70 %
Corn	13 %
Rice	8.6 %
Soy beans, kidney beans, chick peas, lentils, etc.	10 - 35 %
Almonds, walnuts, cashews, hazel nuts, pine nuts, etc.	14 - 30 %
Pumpkin seeds, sesame seeds, sunflower seeds, etc.	18 - 24 %

- Concentrated multi-vitamin tablets/capsules are also a good source of vitamins, minerals and anti-oxidants.
- Fruits and vegetables are full of vitamins, minerals and anti-oxidants and contain high-quality fiber for maintaining good health and a long life.
- The recommended daily allowance: 50 grams of protein (Average adult).
- Calcium from vegetables is more absorbable than from cow's milk.

- To diminish the real threat of a worldwide pandemic from bird flu,
- To avoid the danger of mad cow disease (BSE) and pig disease (PMWS), etc.
- To stop the continuing gruesome sacrifice of billions of our sweet domestic animals, marine life and feathered friends daily,

It's wise to change to a vegetarian diet for good.
It's Health
It's Economy
It's Ecology
It's Compassion
It's Peace
It's Noble

Long Life to You!

Thank You for Your Compassion

For more information, please refer to the websites listed below:
http://AL.Godsdirectcontact.org.tw/   or e-mail to AL@Godsdirectcontact.org
http://www.vegsoc.org/   http://www.vrg.org/   http://www.vegsource.com/
Supreme Master Television, airing only positive programming, will bring a new dimension into your life.
Available worldwide as 24-hour live Internet TV at:
http://suprememastertv.com/webtv/

The Noble Wilds

Author:
Supreme Master Ching Hai

Cameramen:
Supreme Master Ching Hai / Thomas Lerning/ T. Hao/ T. June/ Steve Andreas/ Jus-se / T. Khai

Design and Layout:
Kim Joung Eun, Gary Lai, Annie Yu, Jackie, Cuties, Pearl Huang, Nadir Yen, Eve Lin

Graphic Design:
Gary Lai, Kim Joung Eun, Wang Bor Tang, Yu Hui-Chun, Nadir Yen

Copy Proofreading:
Jane Chu, Lynn McGee, Grace Chen, Sun Wang

Publisher:
Love Ocean Creative International Company, Ltd.
Address : (10664) B1., No. 3, Alley 30, Lane 78, Sec. 2, Fusing S.Rd., Taipei City, 106, Taiwan, R.O.C.
Tel : 886-2-2706-5528   Fax : 886-2-2705-6288
www.loveoceancreative.com / E-mail: info@loveoceancreative.com

The Supreme Master Ching Hai©2008
First Edition: Feb. 2008
Second Edition: Mar. 2008
Printed in Formosa
ISBN : 978-986-84152-3-2 (paperback)
ISBN : 978-986-84152-2-5 (hardcover)